THE LITTLE BOOK OF CHAT-UP LINES

Jake Harris

summersdale

THE LITTLE BOOK OF CHAT-UP LINES

First published in 2011 as *The Little Black Book of Chat-up Lines and Flirting*

This edition copyright © Summersdale Publishers Ltd, 2015

Illustrations © Shutterstock

Summersdale Publishers Ltd
46 West Street
Chichester
West Sussex
PO19 1RP
UK

www.summersdale.com

Printed and bound in Malta

ISBN: 978-1-84953-772-8

Substantial discounts on bulk quantities of Summersdale books are available to corporations, professional associations and other organisations. For details contact Nicky Douglas by telephone: +44 (0) 1243 756902, fax: +44 (0) 1243 786300 or email: nicky@summersdale.com.

Contents

Introduction..5

The Art of the Opener.......................................6

GSOH...11

A Touch of Class..17

Speed Seduction..22

Classic Romantic...32

Golden Oldies..39

The Perfect Ten...44

Killer Put-downs..48

Location, Location, Location...........................51

Body Talk...55

Virtual Lady-land...59

Hollywood Style...72

Getting Physical..74

Down and Dirty..77

Cringeworthy Gems...81

The Great Escape..85

And Finally... Just for Laughs.........................89

Introduction

**'Twenty-ton penguin!
Well, I had to break the ice somehow...'**

'Can I buy you a drink?' is all very well if you're into the whole brevity thing. 'What's your star sign?' could get you into a seriously boring conversation. If you've ever been surrounded by hotties and were stuck for an opening line, this cheeky little guide to getting started with the opposite sex will ensure you never miss an opportunity again.

To be young, free and single has its benefits, but if you're reading this book then you've already decided to risk giving up all that – whether temporarily or permanently – for some action, or at least interaction, with the fairer sex. You can worry about who hogs the duvet and leaving the toilet seat down later on.

Oh, sorry, you're after a quick shag? Well, you may want to skip ahead to the more direct approach later in this book...

THE ART OF THE OPENER

A chat-up line is simply intended to show that you are attracted to a person and to get their attention. Often the line itself is incidental to starting the conversation. The good thing about the subtle approach is that you're not actually chatting her up – you're just talking, right? And if, up close, you realise she's not the hottie you thought, you're safe to escape...

Conversation Starters

A chat-up line that falls flat can leave you red-faced with embarrassment. If someone thinks they're being chatted up, chances are they may put up barriers. You may have more success if you start by asking a question. A non-threatening question may lead to a conversation. If you can ask about something she's reading or wearing without overstepping the bounds of politeness, so much the better. Or you could try opening with a piece of trivia... Read the paper and pick out one fact that you find interesting, and use it to open a discussion.

'I think there's something wrong with my phone. Could you try calling it for me to see if it rings?'

....

'Do you know what's the best thing about being single? Being able to talk to you.'
(This might get you into a conversation – and if she's not single, you'll find out pretty quickly!)

....

'Excuse me, are you accepting applications for your fan club? Because I'd like to join.'

....

'You're so beautiful you've probably heard every chat-up line in the book.'

....

'I have a phone and you have a phone number... think of the possibilities!'

"NICE TO MEET YOU, I'M [NAME]. AND YOU ARE... GORGEOUS! "

'I would guess you're against hunting –
am I right? Because you're a fox!'

·······································

'Let me introduce myself –
I'm your future husband.'

·······································

'I've had a really bad day and it always
makes me feel better to see a pretty girl
smile. So, would you smile for me?'

·······································

'I'm going to get in touch with the
Ordnance Survey people to let them know
I've found an Area of Outstanding
Natural Beauty.'

·······································

'What's a lovely person like you
doing around people like me?'

GSOH

Making someone laugh is half the battle – everyone knows that a good sense of humour is high up on a woman's wish list. Generally women find witty men very attractive, and using a funny chat-up line also shows confidence, another characteristic women like in a man. If you can make a woman laugh, then you are definitely on to a winner! Just make sure you perfect the art of delivery...

Gift of the Gab

Approaching a member of the opposite sex who is a complete stranger is a tough thing to do. You need to get talking. Even if you're the very embodiment of charm and have looks that could kill (or at least maim!) at ten paces, if you can't make a person feel comfortable talking to you then the chances are it won't lead to seeing them again. If the person likes you, they'll want to keep the conversation going – it's just knowing where to start.

'Are you from Tennessee?
Cos you're the only ten I see!'

....

'Is this the Starship *Enterprise*?
Because you are out of this world!'

....

'You must be Jamaican...
because Jamaican me horny!'

....

'Sorry to bother you but I suffer from
amnesia. Do I come here often?'

....

'Do you have any raisins?
How about a date then?'

....

'Hi, I'm a postman, so you can rely on me
to deliver a large package.'

**IF YOU HAD
A LADDER IN
YOUR TIGHTS,
IT WOULD BE A
STAIRWAY TO
HEAVEN.**

'I've got this brilliant new watch with a special sensory device that tells me you're not wearing any underwear!'
'Nice try. I am wearing underwear.'
'Ah, I must reset it – it's obviously an hour or so fast.'

....

'I know I'm not the best-looking bloke here, but beauty is only a light switch away.'

....

'Your eyes are the same colour as my Porsche. And yes, they're both things I've only seen in my dreams.'

....

'My friend thinks you're beautiful, and if it's any consolation so do I.'

The Wingman

Women often enjoy the witty banter of two men, which can seem less aggressive and awkward than the targeted approach of one. A good strategy is to bring along a mate (preferably an ugly one!) to get the conversation started, but make sure she realises he's the clown and you're the sensitive one.

A TOUCH OF CLASS

Most people like to be made a fuss of, and while being upfront can work for some, it might also pay to show a little sophistication and to hit your target with something that will stimulate their mind as well as their G spot. Flattering someone with witty lines and romantic gestures shows that you could be a keeper.

The Old-fashioned Romantic

You're a modern guy, you want to find yourself a modern girl... naturally you're going to look to the latest technology to help you find, and hopefully keep, the perfect partner (see p.59). But don't overlook the benefits of old-fashioned romantic traditions – they've been wooing girls successfully for centuries. Cook her a candlelit dinner, make her a mixtape (the proper way – yes, that means burning her favourite songs on to a CD, not giving her an iTunes voucher), write a poem or love letter, or turn up on her doorstep with flowers and chocolates – they may be clichéd but you can rest assured she won't be turning any of these things down!

Literary Lines

Love is a temporary madness.

Louis de Bernières

....

The only true gift is a portion of yourself.

Ralph Waldo Emerson

....

The course of true love never did run smooth.

William Shakespeare

....

There is only one happiness in life: to love and be loved.

George Sand

....

Love is composed of a single soul inhabiting two bodies.

Aristotle

"

WHO EVER LOVED, THAT LOVED NOT AT FIRST SIGHT?

"

Christopher Marlowe

There is no instinct like that of the heart.

Lord Byron

....

Never close your lips to those whom you have already opened your heart.

Charles Dickens

....

Kisses are a better fate than wisdom.

E. E. Cummings

....

Love is the only gold.

Alfred, Lord Tennyson

....

Love is most nearly itself when here and now cease to matter.

T. S. Eliot

SPEED SEDUCTION

Someone once wrote that men are sexual bulldozers, while women are sexual window boxes, and if you try to tend a window box with a bulldozer... Then again, sometimes the more direct approach is worth a try.

Successful Speed Dating

From its humble beginnings in California in 1998, speed dating has become one of the most popular ways to find a potential partner. Be natural – you want to appear interested (and interesting), but don't lay it on with a trowel and declare your undying love. Instead, pay a compliment, but make it one that is genuine, and don't act out of sorts in an attempt to be memorable. On the flip side, avoid asking dull questions – although small talk is the easiest way to make conversation under pressure, you certainly won't make a lasting impression.

Speed-dating Etiquette

 Dress to impress – a good impression is the key to successful speed dating, so make sure you look the part as well as act the part.

 Don't go to the event drunk – you might think you're the poetic equivalent of Shakespeare, but all they can hear is a babble of words.

Make an effort to smile – they are all in the same boat as you!

Avoid work talk – unless you're a magician or an astronaut, a description of your job role isn't the most fascinating thing to discuss with a potential partner when you first meet them (even if you think otherwise).

 It's not all about me, me, me – if you notice yourself answering a lot of questions, try to ask some in return. If you're attracted to the person, you need to look like you're interested.

 Don't waste time speaking to someone you don't fancy after the event – excuse yourself politely before they start to think that they have a chance.

Avoid a Tumbleweed Moment

When you're looking directly into the eyes of a stranger and you're expected to talk for a certain length of time, panic can strike and leave you speechless. To save you from moments like these, memorise some of the following questions to make you seem like the cool and composed guy that you'd like to be:

 Where did you grow up?

 Do you have any brothers or sisters?

 Do you have any pets?

 Where was the last place you travelled to?

If you could go anywhere, where would it be?

 What do you like to do on your days off?

What's your favourite meal?

 What's the most adventurous thing you've ever done?

 How would your best mate describe you?

 If you could meet anyone, who would it be?

 If you had a superpower, what would it be?

Cutting to the Chase

If you're looking for a long-term lover, turning on the charm tactics and slowing down the pace is the most common way to succeed in your pursuit for love. However, there are times when lust outweighs love, temptation overrules abstinence, and all you want is to get down and dirty.

(Not recommended for speed dating, just for when you're feeling impatient and a little cheeky!)

'All those curves, and me with
no brakes…'

....

'You must be a human light switch –
every time I see you, you turn me on!'

....

'I always had trouble learning the
alphabet. I think U and I should
be together.'

....

'Do you have to have a special licence
for that? For driving me crazy?'

....

'Do you know the difference between sex
and conversation? Want to talk about it?'

"
GET YOUR COAT – YOU'VE PULLED!
"

'Sorry if I'm wrong, but don't you want to kiss me?'

....

'Do you sleep on your stomach? Can I?'

....

'How would you like your eggs in the morning? Fertilised?'

....

'Is that a mirror in your pocket? Because I can see myself in your pants!'

....

'Let's get something straight between us.'

CLASSIC ROMANTIC

Romance and compliments are still important – perhaps now more than ever – and many women will give you credit for being romantic, as long as you are honest. Try to say something specific about her appearance, but if one of these lines can make her laugh first then so much the better...

Manners from a hundred years ago sometimes hold true today:

Court Scientifically

If you court at all, court scientifically. Bungle whatever else you will, but *do not bungle courtship*.

Speak Correctly

Remember that all 'slang' is vulgar. It has become of late unfortunately prevalent, and we have known even ladies pride themselves on the saucy chic with which they adopt certain cant phrases of the day. *A gentleman should never permit any phrase that approaches to an oath to escape his lips in the presence of a lady.*

Up and At It

Dress up, spruce up and be on the alert. Don't wait too long to get one much more perfect than you are, but *settle on someone soon.*

The Rejected Partner

If a lady should civilly decline to dance with you, making an excuse, and you chance to see her dancing afterwards, do not take any notice of it, nor be offended with her. It might not be that she despised you, but that she preferred another. *We cannot always fathom the hidden springs which influence a woman's actions.*

But if you think you have more of a chance of success by using a trusty chat-up line, here are a few more that could make your desired go weak at the knees...

'They say everything's made in China these days. It's good to see some things are still made in heaven.'

....

'Ow! Sorry about the limp. I hurt my knee, falling for you.'

....

'You remind me of a parking ticket. You've got "fine" written all over you.'

....

'Is your father a thief? Because someone stole the stars from the sky and put them in your eyes.'

"IS YOUR SURNAME JACOBS? BECAUSE, GIRL, YOU'RE A CRACKER. "

'Is that a fox on your shoulder,
or am I seeing double?'

....

'Did the sun come out,
or did you just smile at me?'

....

'I'm thinking of calling the police, because
you stole my heart from across the room.'

....

'Your lips look so sweet – I swear I could
give up sugar for life if I kissed you!'

....

'Is it hot in here, or is it just you?'

....

'Do you believe in love at first sight,
or should I walk past you again?'

Did You Know...?

- Medical experts say you're more likely to catch the common cold by shaking hands than by kissing.

- There are more than 900 varieties of red rose.

- The oldest sex manuals were produced in China 5,000 years ago.

GOLDEN OLDIES

Sure, these lines have been used a million times before, but, as the adage goes, 'if it's not broke, don't fix it'. If you haven't used these tried and tested (results inconclusive) chat-up lines before, it could be that just one will land you with The One...

'Tell me, what's it really like in heaven? Because you must be an angel…'

....

'Apart from being sexy, what do you do for a living?'

....

'Were you in the Guides? Because you really have tied a good knot in my heart.'

....

'Sorry for staring at you – I just want to remember your face for my dreams.'

....

'There must be something wrong with my eyes; I can't take them off you.'

"

ARE YOUR LEGS TIRED? YOU'VE BEEN RUNNING THROUGH MY MIND EVER SINCE I SAW YOU!

"

'I think the police are looking for you…
It's got to be illegal to look that good.'

....

'When God made you, he was
showing off.'

....

'You look like my first wife. Seriously –
my friends are always asking me when
I'm going to get married.'

....

'Excuse me, I'm new around here. Could
you give me directions to your bedroom?'

Just One Look

Women enjoy being admired and one of the sexiest things you can do is simply look. A flattering glance of admiration will make a woman feel special, give her pleasure and be something she'll remember. Sometimes it's best not to say anything right away – keep her guessing for a while.

THE PERFECT TEN

That one person may bring you out in a cold sweat but, unfortunately, there's no such thing as the perfect ten chat-up lines to a woman's heart! But put on a sparkling smile and your most devilish charm, take a deep breath and give it a try with this set of ten...

'Can I have a picture of you so I can show Santa what I want for Christmas?'

....

'You're so hot, you're making me melt.'

....

'Is there a rainbow? You look like the treasure I've been searching for...'

....

'Hurry up! My lips won't kiss themselves.'

....

'Pick a number between one and ten. Wrong! Sorry, you'll have to take off all your clothes.'

"

DO YOU WORK WITH THE AIRLINES? BECAUSE MY HEART IS TAKING OFF.

"

'I hope you know first aid,
because you just took my breath away.'

....

'Life is a big jigsaw puzzle –
and you are the missing piece.'

....

'You looked bored so I thought I'd cheer
you up... I thought my face might make
you laugh.'

....

'Smile! It's the second best thing you
can do with your lips...'

KILLER
PUT-DOWNS

Ouch! Nobody likes to be turned down. Maybe she just doesn't fancy you, or she really is just having fun with her mates, or she has a boyfriend. But maybe it's just a bit of banter, so be ready for a comeback yourself! Forewarned is forearmed...

'I'd love to get into your knickers.'
'There's already one arsehole in there, and that's plenty, thank you.'

....

'Where have you been all my life?'
'I wasn't even born for the first half of it.'

....

'Let's be honest, we've both come here for the same reason.'
'You're right: I wanted to meet someone attractive and interesting. I just haven't seen anyone yet.'

....

'Are you free tomorrow night?'
'No, and you couldn't afford me.'

'When I was a prisoner of war they tortured me on the rack, and it wasn't just my legs they stretched...'

'Clearly they also stretched your imagination.'

....

'You bring me out in a hot sweat.'

'You bring me out in an allergic rash.'

....

'I could get lost in your eyes.'

'Why don't you just get lost?'

....

'You know what you'd look great in? My bed.'

'I would offer to shag your brains out, but someone's clearly beaten me to it.'

LOCATION, LOCATION, LOCATION

A sterling chat-up line isn't going to get you anywhere if the only place you're using it is in front of your bedroom mirror. Knowing where to find the kind of girl you're after is key, so if you're after someone in particular, take some time to consider a likely location. If you're not that fussy, why not try some of these...

Ten Places to Meet Women

1. **Salsa dance classes** – women love to dance and very often there aren't enough male partners to go around at classes.

2. **Activities and events** – whether you're getting physical, or you're going to the theatre or a concert, being in public can be a lot less threatening than being cooped up in a stuffy pub.

3. **Language classes** – remember how sexy a foreign language can sound, and women like men who are interested in the world.

4. **Art gallery cafes** – you don't need to know anything about art to show an interest, and women are much more intrigued by the idea of meeting men in romantic and unusual settings.

5. **Public transport** – if there's someone you see every day and she makes eye contact, find a subtle way to get a little closer and start a conversation.

6. **Volunteering** – if a man is already showing that he thinks about others, it sends out the message that he will care about the woman in his life.

7. **Shopping** – it stands to reason that the more you go shopping, the more women you'll meet. Food shopping is ideal.

8. **Wine tasting** – it's something different and, you never know, she may find it as ridiculous as you do.

9. **Walking the dog** – it doesn't have to be your dog, but make sure you borrow a cute one.

10.

SINGLES HOLIDAYS – YOU'RE AWAY FROM HOME, YOU'RE WITH SINGLE WOMEN... WHAT'S NOT TO LIKE?

BODY TALK

It's not just what comes out of your mouth that can score points with the opposite sex. Aside from the messages your general appearance reveals, there are certain subliminal signals that are given off by your gestures and posture which can indicate whether you're striking the right chord or not...

Is She Interested?

Body language isn't a sure way of 'reading' someone, but it's worth paying attention to it, especially if there's a combination of signs:

 Playing with her hair – touching it unconsciously shows she's at ease in your company.

Being careful about the way she eats or drinks or puts on lipstick – shows she cares about how she looks.

 Adjusting her clothes to make sure they look good – she wants to look her best.

Looking at you and smiling – it sounds obvious, but if she's not doing this there may be something wrong.

 Unintentionally mirroring your actions – there may be a connection between you.

Body Language

The forearm is packed with pleasure nerves that respond best to a touch travelling 1–10 centimetres per second, according to a scientific report in medical journal *Nature Neuroscience*. These 'C-tactile' nerve fibres send signals to the limbic system, an area of the brain associated with trust and affection. So touching or stroking someone's forearm could be just the right move to cross the 'touch barrier'...

Pucker Up

Women are far more likely to want to have sex with you if you're a good kisser. For a first kiss, less is more. Don't transfer too much saliva or choke her with too much tongue. Start gently and initiate the first move, but make sure your breath is fresh!

VIRTUAL
LADY-LAND

Some might say that there's nothing like the real thing, but nowadays it's often easier to meet someone virtually via instant-messaging apps and online dating sites. The rules of online dating are essentially the same, though you need to be ready when it comes to taking it from cyberspace to face-to-face interaction.

Online Dating

Luckily, nowadays you can talk to your friends openly about your online dating life without being laughed at or publicly stoned. If you have yet to discover this way of meeting people, it can be difficult to determine which site is best suited to your needs. If you're in a bit of a muddle, here are some of the most popular traditional and unusual sites available:

The Traditional

Match.com™

eHarmony® **Parship**

Dating Direct

PlentyOfFish™ Lovestruck®

OkCupid

The Unusual

MySingleFriend™
BeautifulPeople
Tastebuds.fm
DoingSomething

Dating Apps

Dating can be done on the go, thanks to the likes of Tinder. Instead of reading the newspaper while you take a dump, you can be searching for love – and they say romance is dead! Can it get any easier than swiping and tapping your way to the love of your life – or just a quick shag?!

'Follow me on Twitter so I can DM you tweet dreams.'

....

'They say online dating is a numbers game – can I get your number?'

....

'You don't know how many times I had to swipe left to find you!'

" HEY, BEAUTIFUL, WILL YOU BE MY TINDERELLA? "

'Roses are red,
Violets are blue,
You swiped right,
So I think we should screw.'

....

'Girl, are you sitting on that F5 key?
Because that butt is refreshing.'

....

'Can I email you at
lovelylady@myheart.com?'

....

'Do you believe in love at first swipe?'

....

'Is your name Wi-Fi? Because I think I can
feel a connection here.'

Creating a Successful Online Dating Profile

You're an easy-going, adventurous guy looking for a woman with a great sense of humour – just like millions of other men out there. No wonder you're getting the dregs from the bottom of the barrel. Here are some top tips to help you write your profile.

 Don't be predictable – if you're struggling to find a synonym, use a thesaurus. If you're struggling to muster up any words at all, look at some template profiles on the internet to start you off.

Resist any emotionally fuelled rants about an ex – no one wants a complainer and everyone has a history.

 Don't be too obvious if you're looking for only 'one thing'.

 Don't say you're a seven-foot, strapping hunk who enjoys shoe shopping at the weekends when it's not true. You'll only feel like a fool when you meet your date.

How to Interpret an Internet Dating Profile Photo

 No photo – looks-wise, I'm more *National Geographic* than lads' mag.

 Oddly positioned webcam photo – I spend at least five hours a day trawling dating websites in between updating my Facebook page.

 Revealing torso shot – don't forget your toothbrush.

 Tattoos and piercings galore – don't forget the TCP.

 Chirpy portrait shot – I'm an agreeable and largely normal person (as far as my photo goes).

Keep it Real

It's so much easier to type out your feelings from a distance on your mobile than it is to express them in a real-life conversation, and it pays to be aware of this and think about exactly what message you're putting across. Does a kiss at the end of a message mean flirting is taking place? Maybe, maybe not... If you're getting mixed signals, the best thing you can do is ask – at least she won't see your face turning red if you've got the wrong end of the stick!

Saucy Smileys (for Those Who Still Text)

There are loads of variations, but here are some classic emoticons that might get you that step further.

The Wink ;)
Cheeky, cheerful and bound to lighten the mood.

The Eyelash Bat ;;)
You're feeling flirty (or you've got something in your eye!).

The Kiss :*
More than your average 'x'.

The Bunny
(V)
(. .)
C(")(")
Something fluffy that is guaranteed to make her smile.

Love-struck :X
For laying it on thick.

The Angel 0:)
Flattery of the supernatural kind.

The Devil >:)
For when you're feeling naughty.

The Rose
@};----
For when you can't afford a real rose.

The Hug >:D<
For when you're feeling lovey-dovey.

The Blush :">
For when you want to play it coy.

The Heart <3
For a romantic touch.

The Tongue :P
Good for being cheeky and for licking.

HOLLYWOOD STYLE

Lots of women are suckers for a good romcom ending – the type of Hollywood climax that involves revelations, rain, tears, kissing and loud dramatic music. If you're getting somewhere but haven't quite sealed the deal, why not go all out and try an overblown gesture as seen on the silver screen?

Draw her portrait à la *Titanic* – if you can get her in the nude then chances are you've already done the hard work!

 Serenade her from outside her window – yes, it's been done to death, but it beats climbing a drainpipe and you're less likely to end up in A & E.

 Share a plate of meatballs and offer her the last one. A cheaper alternative is to offer her your last Rolo.

Look Like a Leading Man

The fairer sex don't want to be accosted by smelly, unkempt men who haven't shaved for five days and look like they've spent the night in a dustbin. Make time to groom and your potential hook-ups may appreciate you that little bit more.

GETTING
PHYSICAL

The devil makes work for idle hands, so why not put
yours to good use and get touchy-feely when you're
flirting? Physical contact while chatting someone
up can be potent – a gentle hand on an elbow while
you're delivering a line has an immediate impact and
can really help to get the message across. Or you
might find success by making a fun game of it – just
make sure it's done with a twinkle in your eye, backed
up with a witty line (rather than simply catching them
unawares!).

Palm-reading

Palm-reading is an ancient art and it can work well in the context of flirting. Asking if you can read a girl's palm gives you the opportunity to take her hand in yours and to run your fingers over her skin. It also gives you the chance to flatter her by saying the lines indicate a 'passionate person, bursting with sexual energy'.

Eyeball Reading

Before going for this tactic, make sure your breath is minty fresh. To perform an eyeball reading, you need to stand nose to nose, staring directly into each other's eyes. Pretend to read the lines of the iris, explaining that someone's perfect match can be determined by the patterns in their eyes — since you're doing the reading, you can simply describe yourself!

Massage

It may be an oldie, but it's a goodie. To be fully prepared, learn some basic techniques of neck and back massage before diving in and accidentally squishing the life out of someone. If a girl mentions they have back or neck pain, it's an ideal opportunity to get busy with your hands, or you could simply mention that you love giving massages.

DOWN AND DIRTY

Let's face it – lots of girls go for the bad boy. Sometimes this means you have to play it cool while sometimes it means you can go all out and be downright dirty. If you get the right girl, being cheeky and a little bit smutty can be a big winner – and a fast track to getting jiggy in the bedroom. 'Many a true word is said in jest' as they say, so if you're rude in a fun way, you're also giving off the signal that you're serious about getting physical. Here are a few chat-up lines that are naughty but nice.

'Do you want to play army? I'll lie down and you can blow the hell out of me.'

....

'I've just received government funding for a four-hour expedition to find your G spot.'

....

'There are 256 bones in your body. Would you like another?'

....

'If you were a lolly, I'd be licking you all night!'

" WANT TO PLAY TV? I'LL PLAY WITH YOUR KNOBS WHILE YOU WATCH MY ANTENNA RISE. "

'Nice shoes. Wanna screw?'

....

'I own the best roller coaster in town –
would you like to ride it?'

....

'Hi. I've been undressing you with
my eyes all night long and think it's
time to see if I'm right.'

....

'I suppose a shag is out of the question?'

....

'I'll show you mine if you show me yours.'

CRINGEWORTHY GEMS

Making an idiot of yourself by using a truly heinous chat-up line is one way to break down the barriers and get a conversation going. However, before you unleash one of these howlers, assess her personality. For instance, if she seems like the bookish type and the line bombs, you can pretend you were being ironic and launch into a conversation about sexual dynamics in postmodern society.

'I'm a meteorologist and I'd like to study your warm front.'

....

'Hello. You don't know me but I've just come back from the future, in which you and I have the most passionate love affair. And it started tonight, actually.'

....

'If I said you had a beautiful body, would you hold it against me?'

....

'There's something on your face. I think it's beauty...'

"

YOU KNOW, HAVING LOTS OF MONEY CAN BE PRETTY LONELY WITHOUT SOMEONE TO SHARE IT WITH.

"

'Do you have a map?
I keep getting lost in your eyes.'

....

'Did you just fart?
Well, you blew me away.'

....

'You're so hot, I bet you're the cause of
global warming!'

....

'Congratulations! You've won first prize in
a competition: a date with me!'

THE GREAT ESCAPE

If you like to engage in a little wordplay, regardless of the consequences, then arm yourself with these put-downs to escape unwanted admirers.

'What's your idea of a perfect evening?'
'The one I was having before you came over.'

....

'You've got the face of an angel.'
'And you've got the face of a saint. A St Bernard.'

....

'I've come from another planet to seek out beautiful life forms.'
'Is that because your race is so ugly?'

....

'I never forget a face.'
'Neither do I, but in your case I'll make an exception.'

....

'When can we be alone?'
'When we're not with each other.'

" SHALL WE GO ALL THE WAY? "

" SURE, AS LONG AS IT'S IN DIFFERENT DIRECTIONS. "

'I think I could make you very happy.'
'Why? Are you leaving?'

....

'How did you get to be so beautiful?'
'I must have got your share.'

....

'I'm sure I've noticed you before.'
'That's funny – I haven't noticed you yet.'

....

'May I introduce myself?'
'Certainly – try those people over there.'

AND FINALLY... JUST FOR LAUGHS

Cheesy lines are high risk but at least they're cheeky, and laughter is better than silence!

'You don't know me, but I dreamt about you last night and thought it only fair to introduce myself.'

....

'You're hot, I'm cool. Maybe if we got together we could even things out.'

....

'Do you know what winks and shags like a tiger?'
'No.'
[Wink.]

....

'Do you have a boyfriend? Well, when you want a man-friend, come and talk to me!'

....

'Want to see my scar?
My circumcision scar.'

"DO YOU KNOW THE DIFFERENCE BETWEEN A HAMBURGER AND A BLOW JOB? NO? LET'S HAVE LUNCH SOMETIME..."

'Did you just look at my bum?'
'No.'
'Oh, that's a shame...'

....

'I'm like a Rubik's cube. The more you play with me, the harder I get!'

....

'There's something wrong with my phone. Your number isn't in it!'

....

'Do you believe in the hereafter? Well, then I guess you know what I'm here after?'

"
MY NAME'S [NAME], BUT YOU CAN CALL ME ANYTIME.

"

'Would you sleep with a stranger?'
'No.'
'Then let me introduce myself properly...'

....

'I'd love to cook you dinner sometime,
on one condition: you cook me breakfast.'

....

'What has 148 teeth and holds back the
Incredible Hulk? The zip on my pants!'

....

'You must be a general, because my
privates just stood up to attention.'

....

'I'll be the six, if you'll be the nine.'

....

'What's a nice girl like you doing in a dirty
mind like mine?'

THEN AGAIN, YOU COULD JUST TRY:

"

SORRY, I KNOW THIS IS A BIT FORWARD, BUT IF I DON'T ASK I MIGHT NOT SEE YOU AGAIN. COULD I CALL YOU SOMETIME?

"

If you're interested in finding out more about our books, find us on Facebook at **Summersdale Publishers** and follow us on Twitter at **@Summersdale**.

www.summersdale.com